REPORT
2022

Stand Up for Human Rights

www.silencedturkey.org

Produced by Advocates of Silenced Turkey Inc. & AST Publishing

TABLE OF CONTENTS

WORDS FROM
THE ADVOCATES

When the Turkish President declared in an infamous speech that "Old Turkey no longer exists. This Turkey is new Turkey", the story of Turkish authoritarianism had once and for all taken on a new character. Since July of 2016, the Turkish government has improperly imprisoned **160,000+** homemakers, teachers, NGO workers, academics, judges, prosecutors and journalists.

Once upon a time, the Republic of Turkey was lauded by insiders and outsiders for constituting a powerful model for democratization. In New Turkey, however, silence against the regime's draconian laws, mass imprisonment, and frequent violations of universal human rights has become the norm.

In a regime which ranks as the worst upholder of the rule-of law including Eastern Europe & Central Asia, 200+ media outlets have been shut down and **308 journalists** and numerous human rights defenders, politicians, including Ilhan Isbilen, Hidayet Karaca, Buşra Erdal, Selahattin Demirtaş and Osman Kavala are held as political prisoners of the state. As a prominent journalist and recipient of international awards, Ahmet Altan was among the political prisoners who resist the regime's unlawfulness. He was jailed for five years as a result of the crackdown on freedom of expression in Turkey.

We are a group of lawyers, judges, academics, journalists, and hundreds of activists who cherish democratic ideals and universal human rights. We are prisoners of conscience wanted by the Erdogan's regime, relatives of political prisoners, and victims who have lost their jobs, property and even family members to the current administration which has been described as a Mafia State. We are the Advocates of Silenced Turkey.

We, the Advocates, have made it our mission to champion the rights of Silenced Turkey until universal human rights and democratic governance are established and sustained as the utmost priorities of the Republic of Turkey. In this regard, we have been the voice of voiceless people of Turkey by means of more than **200 human rights projects.** We have shared the stories of the victims of grave human rights violations and persecution in Turkey through the personal belongings of them in The Social Genocide exhibition held in over 4 locations so far. We are also sharing the lives and experiences of persecuted people of Turkey with books. Among those books are the life stories of Gokhan Acikkollu and Halime Gulsu who died of torture in during incarceration in Turkey's jails. In order to shed light on hideous assaults and rights violations in jails that women face, we have recently conducted a survey which will be reported to international entities and presented in conferences. Furthermore, as AST, we have been gathering prominent human rights experts to only discuss the human rights issues but also recommend solutions at our signature event, the Freedom Convention. For more work we do as human rights defenders please see this report closely.

Thank you for all the support you do to help us achieve our humanity goals!

help@silencedturkey.org

AST GIVES A VOICE TO THE VOICELESS

AST holds conventions to bring light to the ongoing conflict and its influences in Turkey and also develops strategies to champion human rights worldwide through panels, discussions, workshops, art and photo exhibitions, and legal training sessions. Among the events we have organized are the ***Freedom Convention 2022,*** Women as Survivors of Conflicts (within the UN CSW conferences), film festivals, photo exhibitions and book talks! Around **1,880 materials** including; reports, events, infographics and videos have been created in four years.

TAKE ACTION

We stand up for our rights and the rights of others who have been silenced. You can be one of the advocates of silenced Turkey by being a volunteer of AST. You may apply to be a volunteer by emailing **help@silencedturkey.org**

ADVOCATES OF SILENCED TURKEY

Murat Kaval	President and CEO
Hafza Girdap	Executive Director & Spokesperson
Hevin Elmas	Finance Assistant
Nur Cam	APH Project Assistant
Zeynep Caliskan	Finance Assistant
Kubra Sam	APH Project Manager
Ayse Nur	Research Assistant
Meral Hak	Regional Coordinator
Semra Yerli	Regional Coordinator
Eda Kas	Volunteer Coordinator Asst.
Umit Kardes	Regional Coordinator
Murat Has	Regional Coordinator
Yasin Gurel	Regional Coordinator
Osman Abdullah	Regional Coordinator
Vefa Bayir	Regional Coordinator
Abdullah G.	Regional Coordinator
Suheyla Nar	Representative
Vaner Can	Regional Coordinator
Rana Bilen	Graphic Designer
Saime İlker	News Content Manager
Nurettin Kar	Art4HumanRights Coordinator
Betul Iman	Youth4HumanRights Coordinator
Mine Altın	High School Youth Coordinator
Elif Soy	Women's and Children's Rights Coordinator
Muhsin Nazif	Graphic and Web Designer
Hamza Yormaz	Producer
Ayşe Nur	Volunteer Affairs Coordinator
Murat Dogan	Legal Consultant
Joseph Selam	Legal Consultant
Yasemin Kahraman	Legal Consultant
Mustafa Yaz	FaceBook Admin
Serkan Tayyar	Youtube Coordinator
Eyup Guler	Advisory Board Coordinator
Onur Has	Institutional Relations Coordinator
Erkan Erk	Instagram Admin
Bulent Ceyhan	Reporter

Ali Tepe	Scholars Rights Watch Coordinator
Aydogan Vatandas	Media Freedom and Reporter
Esma Birlik	Twitter Manager
Elif Halo	Hope Stories Project Coord.
Ayse Gul	Kahoot Human Rights Contest Coord.
Sermin Is	Regional Volunteer Coordinator
Afra Hur	Translation Coordinator
Rabia Inan	Art for Human Rights Assistant
Sueda Murat	Internship Coordinator
Hilal ince	Survey Manager
Mina Leyla	Author and Reporter
Zeynep Kayadeler	Author

ADVISORY BOARD MEMBERS

Gretchen Eick, Ph.D	Academician
Marra Yates	Undergraduate student/ Staff at a Local Hospital
Karl O'rourke	Chairperson of the Inter-Faith Committee
Kelly Isola	Pastor
Michael Poage	Author
Ann Suellentrop	Nurse & Activist
Taylor Qualls	Pastor/Counselor
Sheri Hays	Social Worker and Human Rights Activist
Stephen Arbeau	Teacher, Activist
Sat Bir	Human Rights Activits/ Non-profit President
Allen Olshtein	Chaplain
Jim Juhnke, Ph.D	Professor of History
Jude Huntz	Campus Minister
Edward Stevenson	Retired Pastor
Bailey Hughes	Legal Consultant
Lewis Hinshaw	Pastor
Gloria Hinshaw	Teacher
Ferhat Ozturk, Ph.D	Refugee and Academician
Psk. Yasemin Milhan	Refugee and Psychologist
Mehmet Halidun, Ph.D	Refugee and Academician

*Some of the names above have been changed due to security concerns of the members whose relatives might be harmed by the current authoritarian regime in Turkey.

FREEDOM
CONVENTION

In a World that Goes Widely Towards Dictatorships
Freedom Convention 2022: Turkey

Human rights refers to all the privileges and rights that an individual has just by virtue of being human; regardless of race, religion, sexual orientation, or other characteristics. Throughout history, different treaties, decrees, and covenants have increasingly take human rights under protection on a global scale. In other words, the concept of human rights is widely institutionalized. International human rights rules require states to guarantee that their citizens have access to human rights and to protect them from any infringements or abuses of those rights. However, the current Turkish government goes beyond simply failing to uphold these duties and denying them by persecuting the people who support and seek out fundamental freedoms like the right to free speech.

"For that matter, those who criticize the government and people in power have been silenced and ultimately punished with prison sentences for almost a decade specifically since the coup attempt in 2016. The dismissals of 130,000+ public servants, shutdown of 200+ media outlets and 15 universities, imprisonment of more than 150 journalists--legitimized through emergency decrees declared right after the aforesaid failed coup--attest the political oppression in Turkey."

AST (Advocates of Silenced Turkey), as an NGO has relentlessly been working since its foundation in 2017 to champion human rights which are harshly violated by the state in Turkey, with the hopes of supporting a reestablishment democratic values.

Deeply concerned about Turkey's government disregarding human rights, as AST, we have been annually organizing The Freedom Convention, since 2020. Remarking on the international covenants, of which Turkey is a state party, this year the convention addressed the arbitrary deprivation of civil and political rights in Turkey and crack down on freedom of expression in Turkey. Participants and experts also discussed the international humanitarian law in today's world and conflict related abuses including Ukraine case and pushbacks in Greece. Thus, as a unique event focused on Turkey, Freedom Convention 2022 brought ongoing violations and persecutions in Turkey to the global attention and provided a platform for strategies and recommendations to end those violations.

DID YOU KNOW?

OVERCROWDED PRISONS DUE TO WITCH HUNT

Total prison inmate population of **314,502** in government-operated detention facilities with a capacity for only **286,797** inmates.

Human Rights Association IHD underlines that there are currently **1,605** sick prisoners in Turkey, **604 of which are critically ill.**

help@silencedturkey.org

FREEDOM CONVENTION

ABDULHAMIT BILICI
Former CEO of
Zaman Newspaper
USA

AHMET NESIN
Journalist & Author
Germany

ALON BEN-MEIR
Senior Fellow at New York
University's Center for Global
Affairs & Senior Fellow at the
World Policy Institute
USA

ALP ASLANDOGAN
Executive Director of
Alliance for Shared Values
USA

JOCELYNE CESARI
Senior Research Fellow at
Georgetown's Berkley Center for
Religion, Peace and World Affairs
USA

KATRINA LANTOS SWEET
President of Lantos Foundation
for Human Rights
USA

KERIM BALCI
Research Fellow & Communications
Officer at London Advocacy, Journalist
UK

KISTEN GOVENDER
Elected Member of South African
Legal Practice Council
South Africa

ARZU YILDIZ
Journalist, Recipient of
Media Ethics Award &
The Bravest Woman Award
Canada

BULENT CEYHAN
Freelance Journalist,
Recipient of Metin Goktepe
Journalism Award
Sweden

BULENT KENES
Former CEO of
Today's Zaman Daily
Sweden

CENGIZ AKTAR
Professor of Political Science
at the University of Athens
Greece

MEHMET EFE CAMAN
Professor of Political Science at
Memorial University
Canada

MICHAEL RUBIN
Resident Scholar at AEI
USA

NATALI AVAZYAN
Human Rights Activist
Turkey

**OMER FARUK
GERGERLIOGLU**
Member of Parliament (HDP)
Turkey

CRAIG SHAGIN
Professor of Immigration Law
at the Widener University
Commonwealth Law School
USA

DAVID KILGOUR
Fellow of the Queen's University
Centre for the Study of Democracy,
Director of the Council for a
Community of Democracies (CCD)
CANADA

EREN KESKIN
Lawyer & Human Rights Activist
Turkey

ESER KARAKAS
Professor of Public Economics at
the University of Strasbourg
France

RABIA CHAUDRY
Attorney, Advocate,
NYT Best Selling Author
USA

SOPHIA PANDYA
Chair of Religious Studies
Department at California
State University Long Beach
USA

SUMEYYA AVCI
Purged Teacher
Turkey

VONYA WOMACK
Director of the Center for
Global Learning at Cabrini University
USA

EUGENE CHUDNOVSKY
Co-Chair, The Committee of
Concerned Scientists
USA

HAKAN YESILOVA
Editor of the Fountain Magazine
USA

HILAL AKDENIZ
Sociologist
Germany

JAMES HARRINGTON
Founder of Texas Civil Rights
Project & Human Rights Attorney
USA

FREEDOM CONVENTION 2020

Among the panelists of the first session in which minority rights and social genocide issue were discussed were Lantos Foundation President Katrina Lantos Swett, Lawyer Mahsuni Karaman, attorney of Selahattin Demirbas (jailed leader of HDP (Kurdish party in Turkish parliament); politician Abdullah Demirbas, Former Mayor of Sur (Kurdish majority populated); Kurdish author and poet Meral Simsek; American Kurdish Network President Kani Xulam and Lawyer Levent Maziliguney form Turkey who closely follows the cases of human rights violations that purged people face.

In the second session of the Convention, crack down on freedom of expression was addressed by Mohamed Shafie Ameermia, Human Rights Expert and Legal Consultant from South Africa; Lawyer and Human Rights Expert Gokhan Toy, and exile Turkish journalists Bulent Kenes and Levent Kenez whose extradition is demanded from the Sweden government by the Turkish government.

Finally the panelists in the last session talked about international humanitarian law in today's world in regard to Ukraine-Rissia war, pushbacks and refugee crisis in Greece and apartheid in South Africa. The speakers were Lyudmyla Koztovska, the President of Open Dialogue Foundation; Tony Pillay, the Executive Director of Law Society of South Africa, Lawyer Anthimos Sideris from Greece and Prof Vonya Womack, the Executive Director of Refugees Unknown Stories Untold.

I would like to share my key takeaways from the Convention by remaining loyal to the speakers' own words:

FREEDOM CONVENTION

MERAL SIMSEK: "Including myself, so many women have been subjected to torture, sexual assaults and rape in Turkey's jails. As Kurdish women we have been experiencing this issue way before the failed coup. However, our fight for freedom is not only for Kurdish women, it is not just for Turkey's women either. Our fights is for women of the world."

ABDULLAH DEMIRBAŞ: "As a Kurdish individual, I was accepted, by the state, as a terrorist kid who should have been beaten when I was 7; I am 57 now and I am accepted as a terrorist who should be killed! I was sentenced to 300 years imprisonment since I have been politically fighting for democracy whereas my son who was an armed guerrilla was sentenced to 10 years."

LEVENT MAZILIGÜNEY: "Unlawfulness in Turkey is not only affecting the direct victims but whole society. Statistics about the unemployment, hopelessness for the future, increasing suicide incidents evidently showcase this situation."

MAHSUNI KARAMAN: "For Erdogan HDP was a barrier to his autocratic goals and arrested the co-chairs of the party. The verdict that ECHR made about the case of Selahattin Demirtas proves not only the human rights violations our cochairs face but also the collapse of rule of law."

KATRINA LANTOS SWETT: "Laws in Turkey, as in other autocratic regimes, are used as proxies to justify the mass purges. The persecution against Kurdish people and Gulen Movement volunteers through the antiterror law is an example for that matter."

FREEDOM CONVENTION

MOHAMED AMEERMIA: "Purged people of Turkey must urge domestic and international mechanisms to generate tangible goals for advocacy. They also must work to transform the society, must work for the sake of transformation and dignity. It's a hard but not an impossible goal. South African example transformed from apartheid is always a beacon of hope."

LEVENT KENEZ: "In the centre of the human rights issues in Turkey is the inexistent of the independence of the judiciary. Since the Ottoman, for the first time one man is ruling the country. Unless the opposition abandons the regime's discriminatory rhetoric it is impossible to tackle this problem."

BULENT KENEŞ: "According to Stanton's theory of 10 stages of genocide, the regime conducted 9 stages put of 10 against Kurdish people, Gulen Movement volunteers and other dissidents. The only remaining act is mass extermination."

FREEDOM
CONVENTION

GÖKHAN TOY: "Since the arbitrary detentions, enforced disappearances, sexual assaults and torture that the Turkish state conducts are systematic and widespread these are all crimes against humanity."

LYUDMYLA KOZLOVSKA: "Naming the war crimes (kidnappings, torture, sexual assaults...) & archiving them are important in order to be able to hold Russia & all individuals who perpetuate these crimes accountable within the int'l humanitarian laws and organizations."

TONY PILLAY: "Survivors of Turkey purge need to have a future vision in terms of rule of law and advocate for this vision, convince the world to accept this vision. Change will ultimately come driven by people!"

FREEDOM CONVENTION

VONYA WOMACK: (Reflecting on a study on women's rights violations under custody & in jails) "91 percent of the participants were arrested during OHAL & were exposed to many serious rights violations within unlawfulness (sexual assaults, ill-treatment…)"

ANTHIMOS SIDERIS: "Because of the gaps or dilemmas around European border protection, states abuse their power and utilize nationalist rhetoric to justify pushbacks. EU must take action against abuses and protect the rights of refugees."

Solidarity and unity amongst and with freedom fighters and all dissidents are critical more than ever in Turkey - where the rule of law is collapsed, the judiciary is not independent and the regime persecutes people visibly and widely. Ekrem İmamoğlu, the Mayor of Istanbul Metropolitan Municipality, was sentenced to 2 years, 7 months and 15 days in prison at the decision hearing on 14 December 2022 of the lawsuit filed on the grounds that he insulted the members of the Supreme Election Board (YSK). Imamoglu was also deprived of the rights defined in Article 53 of the Turkish Penal Code. Additionally, the recent decision of the ECtHR that 82 judges and prosecutors who were detained and arrested after the July 15 coup attempt were unlawfully treated and that compensation should be paid to these people is yet another example of Turkey's widespread oppression. Given these recent incidents; I, once again, would like to highlight that political parties, individual activists and human rights organizations both domestically and internationally should collaborate in resistance against state's repression. The consensus among the speakers of the Convention demonstrates the necessity of solidarity and resilience.

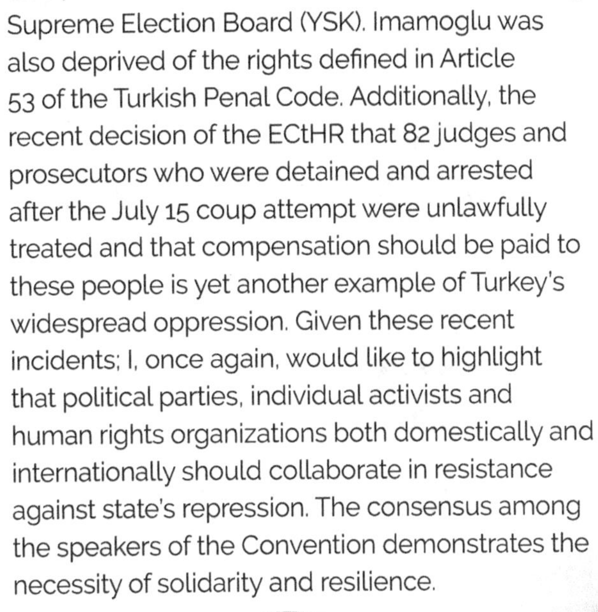

help@silencedturkey.org

REACHED MILLIONS

250,000- 750,000 views per day!

REACHED MILLIONS

silencedturkey

help@silencedturkey.org

FREEDOM TRUCKS

200,000+ MILES in 3 years across 23 states in the USA

silencedturkey

help@silencedturkey.org

FREEDOM TRUCKS

'Stop torture' message on his semitruck is call to action in Michigan's streets

Fatih Yildirim of Schaumburg, Illinois, sits in his 18-wheeler that he owns and calls the Freedom Truck on May 24 in Lansing.
RYAN GARZA, DETROIT FREE PRESS

JAMIE L. LAREAU | DETROIT FREE PRESS | 10 hours ago

Fatih Yildirim is a long-haul truck driver who happens to drive one of the most noticeably shocking trucks on Michigan's roads.

VIGILS & PROTESTS

VIGILS & PROTESTS

STORY OF MUSTAFA KABAKCIOGLU

Mustafa Kabakçıoğlu, a police officer expelled from his job by a statutory decree, jailed

because of his **60 cents donation to KYD a humanitarian organization,** died in a solitary confinement cell in Gümüşhane Prison on August 29 on a **White Chair** when he was just 44 years old.

help@silencedturkey.org

VIGILS & PROTESTS

help@silencedturkey.org

VIGILS & PROTESTS

REPORTS

Torturers Report - 2

According to the report, although receiving applications was restricted in 2020 due to measures against the pandemic, 605 people applied to TİHV on the grounds that they were exposed to torture and ill-treatment. Of the 562 victims, 283 stated that they were subjected to torture in official detention centers and 73 in police stations.

help@silencedturkey.org

REPORTS

Women's Rights Violations by the Turkish Legal System

The intent of this report is to declare the victims of the 'New Turkey,' especially women with children who have been under persecution since the July 15, 2016 coup attempt. Although the Turkish government does not promote transparent data on the number of children imprisoned with their mothers.

Freedom Convention

Turkey Freedom Forum is a unique convention for human rights activists, intellectuals, and policymakers focused on human rights violations in Turkey organized by AST. In pursuance of justice and peace, this forum aims to bring hundreds of human rights defenders and activists together and to foster the dynamics to mobilize. This report will focus on five unique panel topics and will highlight outstanding discussions.

Turkey's Human Rights Record in Numbers

We dedicate this book to all innocent victims of human rights violations, especially to the victims, who lost their lives due to the harsh manifestations of the State of Emergency and Decree Laws.

According to the Global Crime Index report published in 2021, Turkey ranks 1st in Europe in Organized Crime and 13th in the world.

REPORTS

COUP AGAINST JUDICIARY!

THE TRANSFORMATION OF THE TURKISH JUDICIAL SYSTEM AFTER DECEMBER 17-25 CORRUPTION CASES AND JULY 15, 2016 COUP ATTEMPT

The integral principle of democratic regimes, and of a state of law, is the independence and impartiality of the judiciary. As the judiciary is weakened by being exposed to political interventions in countries with weak democratic foundations, it can become a tool of intimidation by dictatorial administrations.

Collapse of Rule of Law in Turkey

There are numerous reports illuminating the collapse of rule of law and the judicial independence in Turkey. The lack of fair trials, the denial of the right to defense, and political interference in ongoing cases summoned close-up scrutiny from international organizations to the nature of post-coup trials, causing debilitating damage to the credibility of trials at all.

DID YOU KNOW?

62,669 POLITICAL PRISONERS

62,669 political prisoners charged with "terrorist activity" At least **686** of them tortured during detention **616** people died under persecution. **61** prisoners died suspiciously **20** prisoners died just in first **9 monthsof 2020** in Turkey.

126 SUSPICIOUS DEATHS

Occurred in detention centers and prisons, according to The Stockholm Center for Freedom (SCF).

REPORTS

https://tinyurl.com/2p9zjee3

Erdogan's Long Arms: Abductions in Turkey and Abroad

It is no secret that Turkey's authoritarian political Islamist regime, headed by the ruling Justice and Development Party (AKP) and its ruler Recep Tayyip Erdoğan, has long been suppressing opposition in the country.

Erdogan's Torture Squads

Government employees who have been involved in the use of torture have been protected by government institutions and officials in Turkey for years and rewarded with impunity. Even when a lawsuit is filed against them, it is ensured that these employees continue their duties and even receive promotions as they are prevented from being sentenced and imprisoned.

https://tinyurl.com/58pbmsrj

https://tinyurl.com/24ntpbhb

Sick and Elderly Political Prisoners in Erdogan's Turkey

The jails in Turkey have long been mentioned in the same breath as inhumane actions and the breach of even the most basic rights, especially against the political prisoners. The violations have reached to unprecedented levels in parallel with the emergence of the current political-Islamist authoritarianism.

ART 4
HUMAN RIGHTS

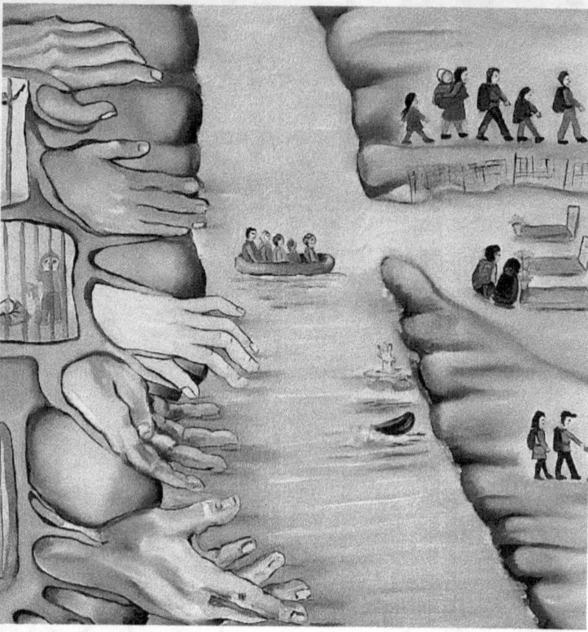

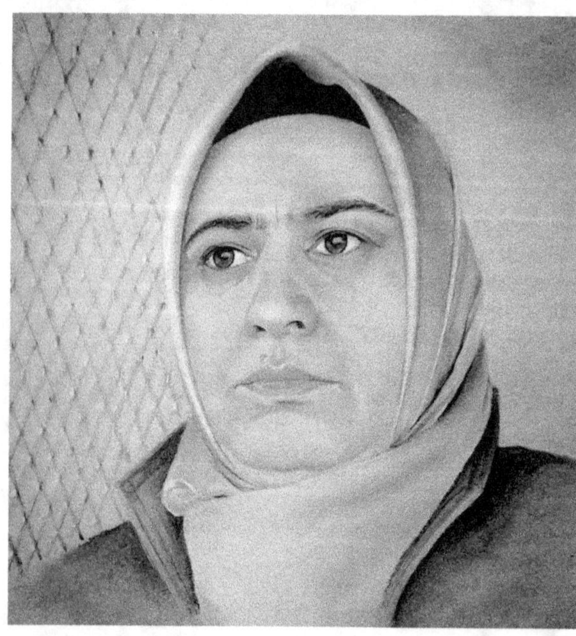

help@silencedturkey.org

ART 4
HUMAN RIGHTS

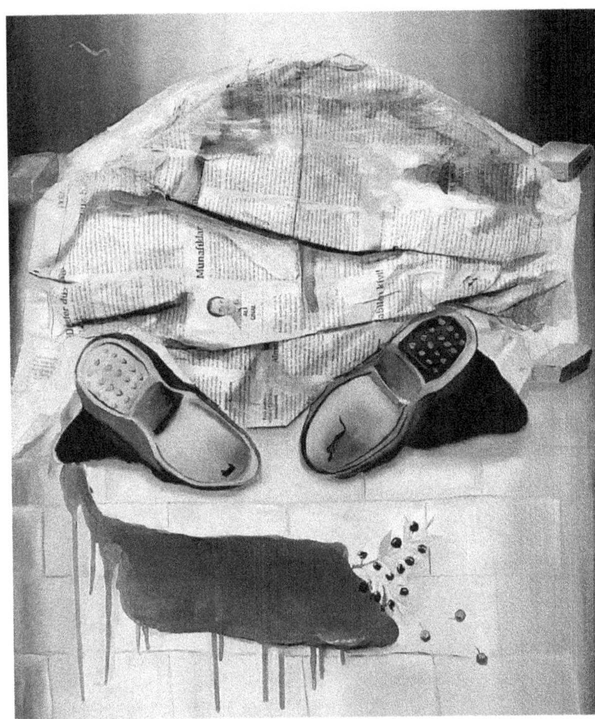

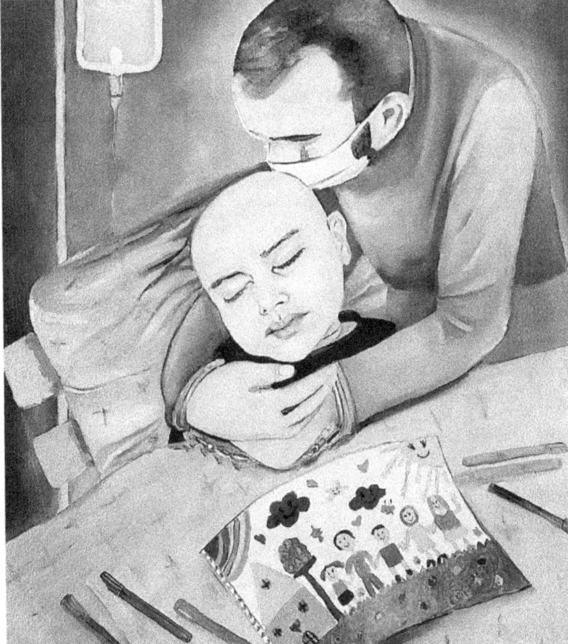

help@silencedturkey.org

ART 4
HUMAN RIGHTS

ART 4
HUMAN RIGHTS

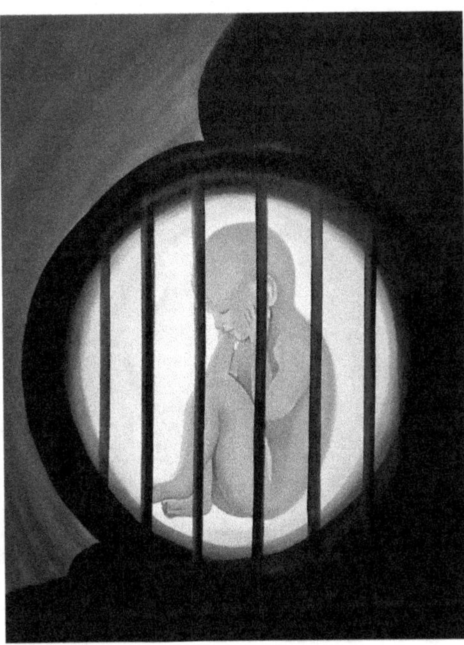

help@silencedturkey.org

BOOKS & PUBLICATIONS

The Life and Legacy of Gökhan Açıkkollu

I will never stop seeking for justice and trying to hold those perpetrators accountable for their crimes, both in this world and the next. I will never say "Well, it is just fate, and there is nothing we can do about it." No, I will not step aside! I will demand justice until justice is done! Yes, I believe firmly in destiny and the Hereafter, but I also believe that if I let those perpetrators get away with their horrendous crimes, shame on me!

The Illustrations of a Teacher in Prison

Yolgezer, a formerly imprisoned artist, invites the world to see the dire human rights violations in Turkey. Through an anonymous activist perspective, the artist specifically depicts Turkey's jails where tens of thousands of political prisoners are kept. You will not only witness how the life is like in prison, but also learn why those prisoners of conscience are incarcerated and how they feel behind bars.

143 Social Genocide Practices in Erdogan's Turkey

This work presents an exhaustive list of flagrant human rights violations to the degree of social genocide, perpetrated after the coup attempt of 15 July 2016. Within this framework, the report identified 143 rights violations and social genocide practices. Since some of these practices are executed publicly, it is known to everyone.

BOOKS & PUBLICATIONS

https://tinyurl.com/4j8aus6c

Stories of Hope 1: Written by Children Refugee and Oppressed

"The Stories of Hope: Written by Children - Refugee and Oppressed" is a compiled selection of the stories submitted for the "Hope Stories from Refugee Children" contest, organized by Advocates of Silenced Turkey (AST) in 2022.

The Life of Halime Gulsu: The Heavenly Teacher Murdered in Prison

They will try to change the reports, the statements, and the facts. They will try to evade taking responsibility. But everyone knows that I was in fact murdered. Those whose hearts have darkened will be proud of their accomplishment.

https://tinyurl.com/5xfdwc3v

Art For Human Rights: Persecution in Turkey

We can't help but speak up... or in this case, sketch up. If you want to help people, you're reminded to say something if you see something. Our voices hoarse, we now turn to pen, pencil, brush, and other media to squeeze out every last word. We at Art for Human Rights organized this collection to present a fraction of the hundreds of pieces from all corners of the world, from artists who wanted not their voices, but their cause to be heard.

https://tinyurl.com/mpr6pa3c

help@silencedturkey.org

SOCIAL GENOCIDE EXHIBITIONS

silencedturkey

help@silencedturkey.org

SOCIAL GENOCIDE EXHIBITIONS

help@silencedturkey.org

SOCIAL GENOCIDE EXHIBITIONS

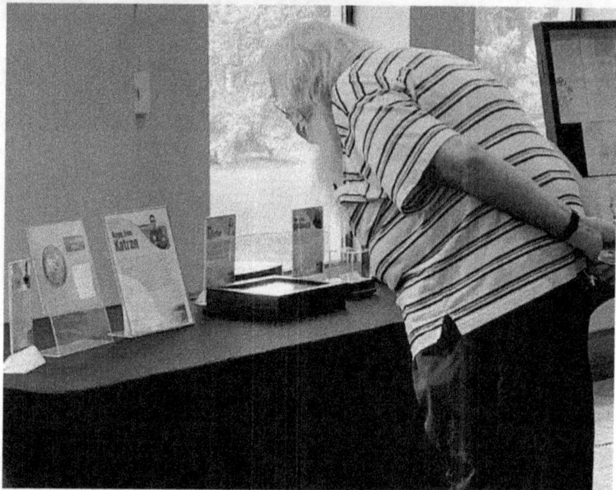

SOCIAL GENOCIDE EXHIBITIONS

help@silencedturkey.org

EVENTS & PROGRAMS

EVENTS & PROGRAMS

EVENTS & PROGRAMS

AST IN THE NEWS

AST REACHED MILLIONS & APPEARED IN THE NEWS 100+ TIMES

TURKEY'S ABYSMAL HUMAN RIGHTS RECORD

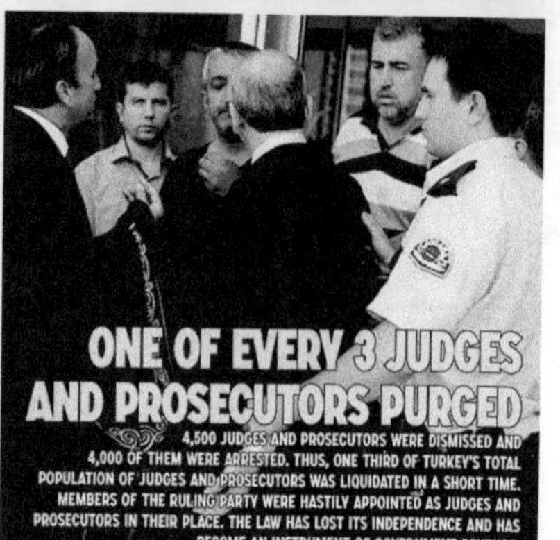

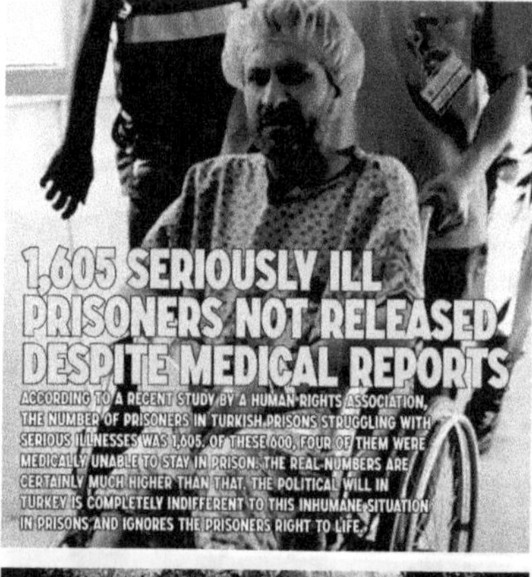

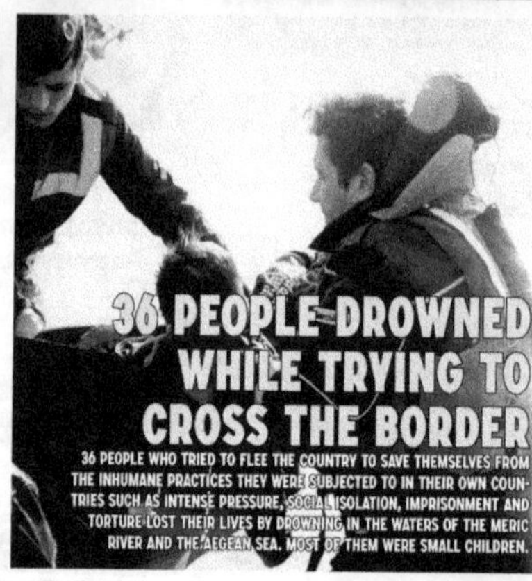

TURKEY'S ABYSMAL HUMAN RIGHTS RECORD

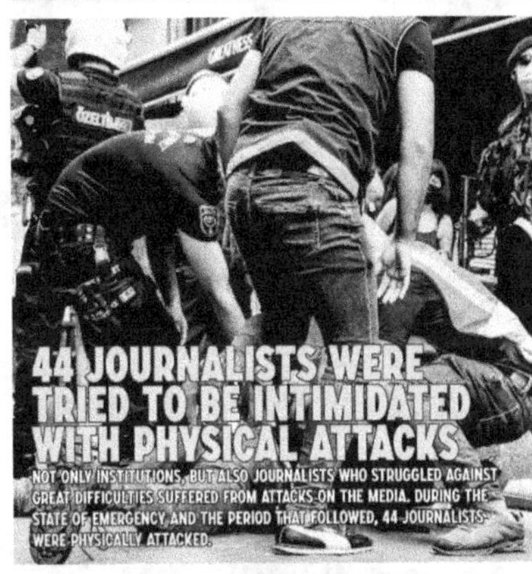

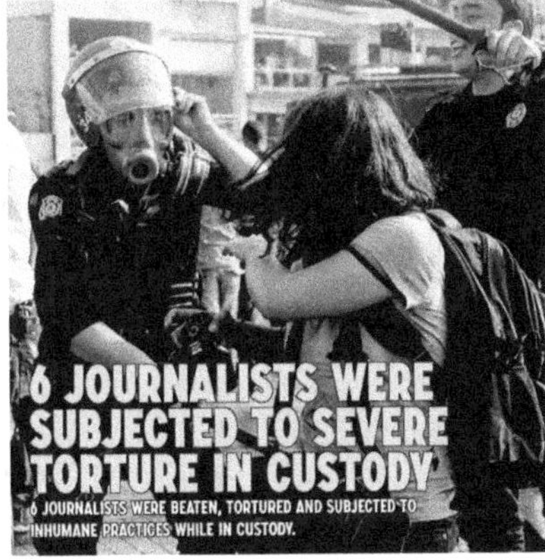

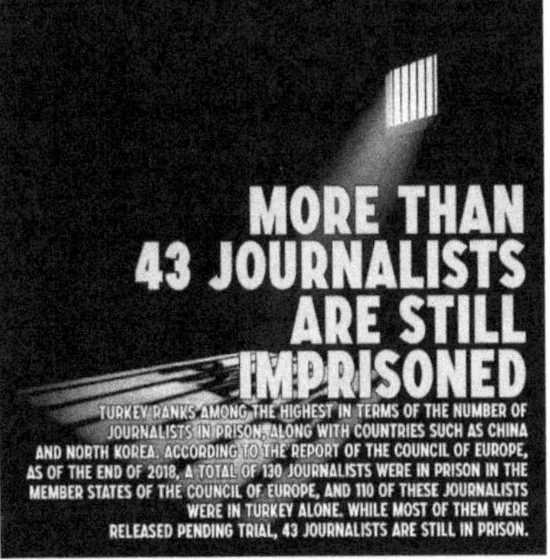

VIDEO CLIPS
& DOCUMENTARIES

Garibe Gezer İşkenceyle Öldürüldü

Social Genocide Exhibition

Justice for Women Protests Press Release

Birader-i Canberaberim / Hikaye

Ah Kalbim / Şiir

Turkey Deserves Democracy, not a Dictatorship! / London Ads

VIDEO CLIPS & DOCUMENTARIES

ABUSE OF INTERPOL BY TURKEY

"HAKKINI HELAL ET ZEKİ..." / HİKAYE

BEN AYŞEMSİZ NE YAPARIM- DOCUMENTARY

ZÜLEYHA'CA / ŞİİR

SENA'NIN UMUT HİKAYESİ

YARGIYA DARBE RAPORU

ANIMATIONS

ABDUCTIONS BY ERDOGAN'S TURKEY

Özlem Meci ve Diğer Mağdur Annelere İthafen

WHAT CAN YOU BUY FOR $1 IN TURKEY? JAIL TIME?

Persecution of Women & Children in Turkey

Mustafa Kabakçıoğlu

Political Prisoners in Turkey and Human Rights Violations

SONGS FOR OPPRESSED

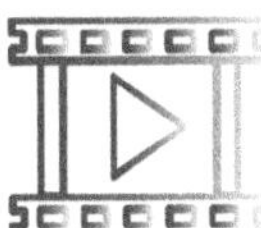

WALKING DOWN / Yağmur Öztürk

SAYFALARCA / OTASKA

SARILSIN ANNEM/ ALP ÇAMALAN

NOLUR/ GRIFON

HOPE/ Yağmur Öztürk

UNUTMAYIN BENİ / BERKUS

 help@silencedturkey.org

TESTIMONIALS

RUTH EFIRD, NURSE, NORTH CAROLINA

I was so surprised to receive the book Silent Scream from you when I came back home yesterday! I had been at my son's home for over 3 weeks. I read it crying last night. My heart goes out to the people of Turkey who are silently protesting the Turkish government.

I signed up for the newsletter so that I can keep up with the latest events.

Thank you for sending me this realistic book of oppression of women in Turkey.

MESSAGE FROM THE MOTHER OF GARIBE GEZER; MURDERED POLITICAL PRISONER GREETINGS FROM MARDIN KENBORAN TO THE US.

You didn't forget my Garibe. You wanted to commemorate her in the exhibition in the US. So I would like to send you a memento of her. I watched and saw your exhibition work, I was very pleased. I know that you have not forgotten and will not forget my Garibe.

Hail to the prisoners, to those in exile. Greetings to all Kurds and Turks. Hello Garibe's friends, comrades, those who have not forgotten her.

You always have a place in my heart. You are always welcome. I would sacrifice myself for you since you don't let my Garibe be forgotten.

And I will never forget you. I will never leave my Garibe's path and I will not forget her.

I will never forget you as long as I live. You are the light to my eyes.
My Garibe was unique. I salute you all.

KARI O'ROURKE

The phrase "a particular bundle of silences" caught my attention immediately. The desire expressed by the group of people who will become the participants in this proposed study is that they want to un-silence their voices. In the fourth proposed group of participants for the study, I will examine more than 40 stories and artifacts of lives that have been lost as a part of Turkish President Recep Tayyip Erdoğan's regime's efforts to eradicate the Hizmet people. I was invited to be a speaker at a social genocide awareness event in New Jersey in June 2022. Afterwards, I organized a group of volunteers to bring the exhibit to Kansas City and in September 2022 we presented the exhibit in three venues and I named the exhibit "Un-Muted." The stories of what -happened to these people are the counter-narratives to what the mainstream media in Türkiye presents. The story of Garibe Gezer is gut-wrenching. She was arrested and sent to prison in 2016 and died in 2021 as the result of prolonged torture, isolation and repeated rape. After we shared her story through the exhibit, her mother sent a video message which the Advocates of Silenced Turkey (AST) volunteers translated to English for us. By sharing Garibe's story we ensured that her voice remains present in the historical record despite the efforts of the dominant regime's attempts to silence it. It is critically important to ensure are not lost to the narrative of dominance and opperession.

help@silencedturkey.org

WHAT WE ACHIEVED

IN 5 YEARS

285

Interviews

36

Books & Stories Published

103

Legal Applications

51

Reports

112

Lectures & Seminars

45

Exhibitions

101
30,000+ attend

Peaceful Protests & Vigils

125

Events & Activities

39

Booklets

120+

AST in the News & Impacts

13

Documentary

73

Take Action & Campaigns

IN 5 YEARS

WHAT WE ACHIEVED

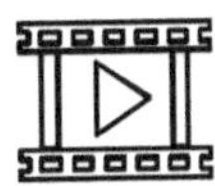

317
Videos & Podcasts

10k+ *attendees*
International Human Rights Conference

200+
Infographics, Flyers & Presentations

10
Petition Campaigns

42+
Press Releases

66
Social Media Campaigns

525+ *art created*
Art & Short Film Contests

200+ *Created per year*
Events and Materials

DID YOU KNOW?

1,477 TORTURE & ILL TREATMENT

The Human Rights Association (HRA) reported that the number of incidents where prisoners were subjected to torture and ill treatment in detention centers and prisons was **2,178 in 2016, 2,415 in 2017, 1,505 in 2018, 1,477 in 2019**

"Archiving Persecution of Hizmet" project records up to **70 victims stories** per year. **241 stories** of victims have been recorded and **35 books published on Amazon and Google Books** so far.

WHERE ARE WE ON SOCIAL MEDIA

Youtube Videos **2 Million+** Viewed

 Twitter — 19.2k+

 Facebook — 60k+
5 FACEBOOK PAGES IN 5 LANGUAGES

 Instagram — 5k+
3 INSTAGRAM PROFILES

 YouTube — 14.9k+

 Email List — 8k+

AST reached a total of **100k+ plus followers** on social media.

silencedturkey

help@silencedturkey.org

VOLUNTEER

If you want to volunteer for AST, please contact us at **help@silencedturkey.org**

We have **705 volunteers** from more than **30 countries**

Total volunteer hours exceeded **16,000**

Social media followers have passed **100k+**

The number of national & international news coverage more than **300**

VOLUNTEERING OPPORTUNITIES

+ **TRANSLATION** (TURKISH - ENGLISH / ENGLISH - TURKISH)

+ **PROOFREADING /EDITING**

+ **WRITING ARTICLES OR ACADEMIC PAPERS**

+ **GOOGLE SEARCH (MEDIA AND DATA ENTRY)**

+ **DESCRIBE VICTIMIZATION THROUGH ART**

+ **FUNDRAISING ACTIVITIES / CALL-CENTER**

+ **INTERVIEWING THE VICTIMS**

+ **INTERVIEW TRANSCRIPTION**

+ **PERSECUTED PEOPLE OCCUPATIONAL GROUPS**

+ **CREATING & SENDING E-MAILS**

+ **CONTACTING CONGRESS & SENATE**

+ **EVENT COORDINATOR**

+ **PUBLIC RELATIONS**

+ **MEDIA RELATIONS**

+ **PUBLIC SPEAKING**

+ **PRESENTATIONS**

+ **GRAPHIC DESIGN**

+ **SOCIAL MEDIA**

+ **VIDEO PRODUCTION**

+ **VOICE RECORDING**

In total, about **1,880 papers,** reports, lectures, events, etc. created by AST. With the power of social media, AST reached millions of people. ▶ Youtube views **2 Million +**

SUPPORT AST

TO CREATE REPORTS, BOOKS, PROGRAMS & MATERIALS TO RAISE THE VOICE OF THE OPPRESSED

The approximate cost to produce reports, books, campaigns, and programs on Human Rights is shown below. ***Thank you for your generous donations.***

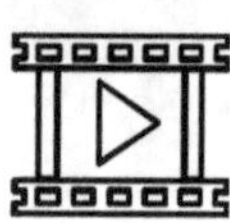

1 Report	$3,000 – $13,000
1 Book on Amazon or Google Books	$6,000 – $15,000
1 Booklet	$750 – $2,000
1 AST Paper	$150 – $300
1 Story	$1,000 – $2,000
1 Infographic	$150 – $300
1 Presentation	$200 – $500
1 Flier	$50 – $100
1 UN Application	$2,000 – $4,000
1 Official Letter Creation	$100 – $250
1 Social Media Campaign Creation	$500 – $2,000
1 Newsletter	$250 – $500
10 Pages Translation	$150 – $400
1 Short Video Production	$1,000 – $3,000
1 Documentary	$4,000 – $20,000
1 Lecture	$1,000
1 Panel	$1,500 – $2,500
1 Exhibition	$1,000 – 7,000
1 Conference fees	$100 – $500
1 News translation	$30 – $100
10 Calls and follow up	$100
10 Emailing and follow up	$100
1 Page translation	$15 – $100
500 Reports printing and mailing	$2,500 – $3,500
1 Song Contest & Award Ceremony	$10,000 – $14,000
1 Art Contest & Award Ceremony	$6,000 – $10,000
1 Short Film Contest & Award Ceremony	$12,000 – $17,000
1 Photo Contest and Award Ceremony	$7,000 – $10,000
1 Animation Cost	$2,000 – $3,000
International Freedom Convention	$20,000 – $30,000
Organizing a Protest	$1,000 – $7,000
Giant Billboard Advertisements	$7,000 – $50,000
Social Media Advertisements	$100 – $5,000
1 Freedom Truck Advertisement	$7,000 – $10,000

silencedturkey

help@silencedturkey.org

SUPPORT AST

by making a monthly donation or one-time donation

☑ **CREDIT CARD OR DEBIT**
silencedturkey.org/donatenow

☑ **PAYPAL**
paypal.me/ast111

☑ **ZELLE**
advocatesofsilencedturkey@gmail.com

☑ **PATREON**
patreon.com/advocatesofsilencedturkey

☑ **SEND CHECK**
Please make your checks payable to
"Advocates of Silenced Turkey"
Address: Advocates of Silenced Turkey
P.O. Box 2399 Wayne, NJ 07474-2399

☑ **SUBSCRIBE TO OUR NEWSLETTER**
https://bit.ly/2UEYDwD

silencedturkey

help@silencedturkey.org

Help us spread the word,
be part of the change!
Together we can help be the voice of the
voiceless people of Turkey.

By making a monthly donation or one-time donation
www.silencedturkey.org/donatenow

By becoming a volunteer
www.silencedturkey.org/get-involved

silencedturkey

help@silencedturkey.org

HOW CAN YOU HELP?

By following us on social media

www.twitter.com/silencedturkey

www.facebook.com/silencedturkey

www.instagram.com/silencedturkey

www.youtube.com/AdvocatesofSilencedTurkey

silencedturkey

help@silencedturkey.org

www.silencedturkey.org

- www.twitter.com/silencedturkey
- www.facebook.com/silencedturkey
- www.instagram.com/silencedturkey
- www.youtube.com/AdvocatesofSilencedTurkey